Poets' Corner
2022

The Bayside Writers' Group

Copyright © 2022
The Bayside Writers' Group
All Rights Reserved
ISBN: 978-0-6489459-9-4

This publication may not be reproduced, stored in a retrieval system, or transmitted in whole or in part, in any form or by any means, electronic, mechanical, photocopying, recording, or otherwise without the consent of the author(s). Inquiries should be addressed to the publisher.

Published in Australia
Printed by Ingram Spark

Poets' Corner 2022

Authors: Amanda Divers, Ann Simic, Judith Dowling, Lucy Tomov, Peter Levy, Rahaf Al Maalouf, Rama Al Maalouf, Rose Lumbaca Crane, Roslyn Evans, Sandra G Lanteri, Suzanne Siebert.

Design: Sharon Hurst

Acknowledgements:

I would like to thank all those who took the time to submit their works to us, especially in these difficult times.

Please note that if anyone would like to make contact with any of the poets in this collection that the best way would be to either post a letter:

The Bayside Writers' Group
22 Stradbroke Avenue
Brighton East, Victoria, Australia 3187

Or email:
baysidewritersgroup@bigpond.com

Contents

Amanda Divers
- Return to self 1
- Sombre sleep 13
- Still waters 26
- Summertime 26

Ann Simic
- A villanelle for Archie Roach (1956-2022) 2
- Numinous 14
- The key 27

Judith Dowling
- Clever Dick 3
- Tea-leaf message 15
- Great Aunt Oriel's ashes 28
- The Brussels sprout 40
- The ever monster 46

Lucy Tomov
- Apology 4
- Artist's fight 16
- Morning noise, upstairs 30

Peter Levy
- A muffled scream 5
- Lloyd's 17
- Vacant blocks 31
- A neighbour's regret 39
- Custodians 48

Rahaf Al Maalouf
- Karma 6
- Pain 18
- She is not just 32

Rama Al Maalouf
- Starry night 7
- The wise tree 7
- When 19

Rose Lumbaca Crane
- Cat with wings 8
- Intuitive bird 9
- My father's tool 20
- My unkempt hair 33
- Time on roofs 42

Roslyn Evans
- A pair of haiku 10
- Lockdown lament 10
- Whitehorse Orchestra strikes up again 22
- Red brick walls 34
- Rhapsody on old lovers 43

Sandra G Lanteri
- The weight of love 11
- The silence of water 24
- On the way to the Tate Modern 36
- Trampoline 44
- Want 50

Suzanne Siebert
- I saw a cloud 12
- These embers 12
- Is there freedom 12
- Travel on 21
- Waters to the sky 38
- Senses 52

Return to self

Let it be known
I no longer feel alone
I refuse to hide
You won't see me cry
Life is for the living
I remain driven
I see only one goal
I will remain moral
Finally found my feet
My soul won't face defeat
I indulge in my wealth
My return to self

Amanda Divers

A villanelle for Archie Roach (1956-2022)

Ripped from your family to trauma and pain
too soon we weep for you who
sobbed your stolen youth from every vein.

At fifteen years your foster home became
a place to flee to find your truth —
ripped from your family to trauma and pain.

Living rough, fights, near insane,
sleeping in bushes, trauma anew,
you sobbed your youth from every vein —

until your Ruby came to sustain you
with love you cherished, with love you knew —
ripped from your family to trauma and pain.

Tumbling through the driving rain
that had always whipped through you,
this gem is what you gained.

Your music flowed, a deep refrain —
fans multiplied thrived and grew;
ripped from your family to trauma and pain,
you sang your stolen youth from every vein.

Ann Simic

Clever Dick

He likes to defy his mortality -
His trust's in his tattoos and sunnies
When he's behind the wheel.
Wherever he goes he's gotta go fast
So he roars with his mighty throttle
And scares old ladies off the road
With his blatant hugeness
His red-faced rudeness.
Teasing with flashing lights
Blasting his horn as he revs
To tell you he's king of the road
As he burns rubber and gas
And churns the miles
Ignoring the leers
He grinds his gears
Booming through
Fuming hate
And running late
Hurrying to get there
So he can hurry again
To hurrying.

Judith Dowling

Apology

I cut myself in cookie shapes.
Sinew spread
across the kitchen bench
the threads purple and violent

holding
the fiery urchin in the
hollow of my chest
it cries and spits
shaking in fits

at the putrid smell
which slicks inside the cracks.
There is a terrible sickness here
about which the cosmos couldn't
care.

Why then,
do you?

Lucy Tomov

A muffled scream

I heard the muffled scream and stayed silent
The sounds of the night lingered in the air
Creaking of boards and strange noises persisted
I filtered them, one by one, with familiar care.
An animal or two rushing from roof to roof
A bird walking squeakily above my window
I noticed the shadows as the moon beams wandered
There was comfort in the leaves of the ageing willow.
Snug under fleecy soft blankets that held safety
Some resonances were accustomed and I felt warm
An odd drop of rain splashed gently and echoed
I wondered if it meant the onset of a winter's storm.
My ears strained to hear more distant human tones
But the muffled scream of hours before was nowhere
There were fridge mutterings and waterpipe grumbles
As I drifted in dreams beyond worry on a prayer.

Peter Levy

Karma

Noise, noise everywhere
I feel no oxygen in the air.
Do not blame me if I scream in a cold vacuum.
Do not interrupt me when I dream in a dark room.
I am now lost in a strange sky, like a stray cloud.
Searching for me, for the previous serenity, for the old sound.
No one is here, no enemies, no peers.
Just bodies chasing illusions with fears.
Just tired souls sunk in their tears.
Where is the sun?
Where is the golden ray?
How dare they steal the hope and run?
Hey, hold on there is a price to pay.
There is a price to pay . . .
for every stolen future.
 for every stolen part.
There is a price to pay . . .
for all the broken memories.
for every broken heart.
Even if you cheated in the game and won the first round.
Even if the rules are changed and the juries were murdered.
Don't worry, karma will eventually come around.
because the voice of the right is always remembered.

Rahaf Al Maalouf

Starry night

Starry night . . . starry night
And the reflection of your light
Makes me sing a sweet song
Reminds me of when I was young

Oh lonely star I see your past
Like your light was born to last
Oh I know you want to change it
But you know if you erase it
You wouldn't be what you are
In the sky a beautiful star

The wise tree

It's that feeling coming back again even when I think
I've won
Like I have an incomplete puzzle within me stopping me
from going on
I sat on the sand peacefully and asked the wise tree for
advice
I said "What should I do tree, please make me more
wise"
She said "Darling, you can only find the answer within
you
Because it's always there waiting like you always knew
Maybe you are looking for your missing piece in the
wrong place
And always remember that finding the ultimate answer
isn't the case"

Rama Al Maalouf

Cat with wings

What is it like sometimes to dance like a cat without a care in the world? Like a cat stretching, expressing its playfulness
The cat knows it's the queen of the jungle the urban jungle
It moves and plays games to get its feed
It is the cat's domain
Claiming its rights with an attitude of pride and confidence
Moving and dancing like a cat, prancing, gliding with elegance
A shiny slick black cat but with wings, as it learnt to fly
Why would a cat have wings? Well wouldn't you want wings?
Oh how much fun being like a cat, a cat with wings
With large padded paws understanding the secrets of this land, for it understands its rhythms
and feels its way through the night

So I dance and move like a cat, planting my feet with purpose and intent, understanding the
laws of cause and effect
From fast to slower and the times it needs to play as it goes about its business and life
Sensing and knowing as the black cat knows what it needs to survive
Through the darkness of night, through the spaces of the in-between worlds
Leaving its imprint while I sleep, making its presence felt through my dreams, hints of visions

and whispers of wild natural healthier ways of being
that is better for me and thee
How much fun I have moving and dancing like a cat, a
cat with wings.

Intuitive Bird

I see the bird high above
High above the sky flying with wings I wish I had
The bird had landed from its flight in the dead of night
So elegantly and gradually closing its wings
From open to thinking in new ways of living and being
as it knows
It knows what is better for you, better for the ones you
love and the ones that are a challenge to love
For new ways of living and being is a challenge at times,
like mastering the mind and body
As an intuitive bird it seems so right
To observe and learn like a bird, an intuitive bird while
high on the highest post
To see what comes about after contemplating,
conversing and doing for that is how we learn
to be like the intuitive bird
The wiser, the happier bird while observing the obvious
and the subtlest
I see the bird high above, I see the intuitive bird within
my heart.

Rose Lumbaca Crane

A pair of haiku

Bluebottles, rainbow
Autumn sun glints on white foam
Moggs beach eroding

Small hooded plovers
Scurry across water's edge
Until dogs take them

Lockdown lament

Sandringham ghost trains flash past.

School bells are silent.

Playgrounds miss their children's laughter.

Skin yearns for its watery caress at my local swimming pool.

Wattles' pungent fragrance greets me as I turn a corner on my solitary cliff top walk.

A bitter taste of loneliness lingers in my mouth.

Roslyn Evans

The weight of love

Once upon a time
a gift from the heavens
in the form of a white balloon
landed at my front gate

I added a bright red ribbon
to make it extra special
and regifted it to Imogen
my grand-daughter of tender months
It gave us much shared delight

The very next day
she uttered her first sentence
Nanna give it

Strange how this lightest of gifts
became the catalyst
that propelled her along her path
towards independence

A year later
on Mother's Day
she placed before me her return gift
This is for you, she said
It's a stone, a flat one

The light   and   the   heavy   of   love

Sandra G Lanteri

I saw a cloud

I saw a cloud that looked like an angel flying,
Which then evolved into a big love heart.
That was precious.

These embers

Your embers ignite my soul
The warmth of every word shared Is embraced in our memory
By my side, kindled and kindred
I carry the light of your eyes In ones that are identical
There is a mix of rest and movement
Of emotion and stillness
And in it all
You are dancing

Is there freedom?

Is there freedom in "after"?
Yes, for those of you who have flight
And when there is no escape from "nothing"
That's when our spirits soar
In the breath of prayer
That calls ...
"Please give me wings".

Suzanne Siebert

Sombre sleep

Sombre sleep
Breath by breath
A once proud Knight ceases to stand
Nothing left but the shell of a man
Self-inflicted and poisoned by life
Hate and anger filled with nothing but spite
Sombre sleep
Breath by breath
Life dwindles down the drain
Tears of former lovers are all that remain
Depression and loneliness are all that surrounds
A heart and soul that craves the sound
Sombre sleep
Breath by breath
The light in life
Shattered by death

Amanda Divers

Numinous

Across the bay, the chilly waters
of autumn equinox meet the
golden will-o'-the-wisp sunset.

The headland juts through the
two, an encroaching monster,
dark and dense, immovable.

In the far distance, the city spikes
misty, with intimations of art and
mystery — harbouring savoir-faire,

luring, tempting, with tasty treats —
mesmerising, teasing, seducing,
turning away from the boundless bay.

I endlessly clasp and cradle both
and feel them spill into each other.

Ann Simic

Tea-leaf message

The roses have withered
Their moisture has morphed away.
Once rife and ripe with burgeoning life
Their heads are bending low,
Petals are falling then shrivelling-
Waiting, like a frail old lady, once dear,
With tissues and talcum in tinder hands
Loose wedding rings on kindling fingers
In a pallid pink bedroom
Where her only view is a window sill
And a curtain, almost closed.

Her hobbled hands encircle a cup
To feel the last of its warmth
Peering in with a rheumy eye
As she watches tea leaves swirl
Then settle onto a tea-leaf message
From a sweetheart never forgotten.
She hears an old tune and sings the words
Of a song they had danced to together
Now freed from its hiding place in her head.
She sings and a smile crinkles her face
Until her cheeks have the blush of a rose.

Judith Dowling

Artist's Fight

Now that you are gone, I write love letters to the moon. I shout at her from the shore, a bewitched and brazen banshee. The house we used to live in is too cold and my feet are weeping blood. The wine glass you threw shattered here, sharpness hiding in the rug your mother made. Those shards separate the woman I was and the man you are. The weeping is confessional now, I hear it from outside me. I am a confession. My breath beats and hardens as it echoes from my trunk.
I realise now that when you looked at me, I folded. I willingly shred myself into fractured contorted figments. Look at me, I am ridding myself of sanctuary for you. I am no longer in my body. You cannot love me; you cannot see me.
You are canvas, paper, sin.

Lucy Tomov

Lloyd's

There used to be a corner shop
That sold all sorts of things
Milk, bread and lots of lollies
And multi-coloured strings.

Mr Lloyd had lost a leg and sat behind the counter
I never saw him on the street
Well, not that I remember.

Each Guy Fawkes Night we'd stare in awe at the crackers on display
Maybe even buy a bag or two
I loved the mighty bonfire in the park around the corner
Sparklers were exciting but skyrockets really flew

One day the shop was boarded up
I saw Mr Lloyd no more
But I fondly kept the memory
Of Mr Lloyd's store.

Peter Levy

Pain

Pain...this burning feeling that has existed since the start of creation.
Pain.. this annoying guest who always comes without invitation.

When it attacks once, you defend, you try to push it away.
Because you do not see the hidden blessing beyond its dark ray.

It heals your forgotten wounds, yet with fire.
It gives you the answer after you deeply enquire.

Every new birth, Every huge change
Every tough victory, every new gain
All of them needed a potion of pain.

Pain is a mindful friend, not a stubborn foe
It gives you priceless wisdom after being raw

Do not hate it, do not resist it
Walk on the road although it is thorny
until you receive the message
Feel it and live the journey

Rahaf Al Maalouf

When

When I see him, everything becomes blurry
Except him with his deep eyes
and the sunlight reflecting on them,
glowing my heart,
Making my soul closer to his.
Suddenly I relax and everything slows down.
And with every time he smiles,
the world becomes more serene.
First time I saw him I was so down
But when he looked at me,
Suddenly I relaxed.
Like he was sent by God to revive my soul.
It's the magic,
When the darkness inside suddenly turns to sunshine.
It is the power of love.

Rama Al Maalouf

My father's tool

The smooth wooden tool that seemed perfect for his hand
His hands were hearty, stocky and robust
Sturdy hands, laborer's hands, hardened by the world's wrongs
Well worn hands that worked the garden
The large well organized garden one of his prides and joy Preparing and planting he did all year round that grew a great harvest for himself and family
Away from the burden and worry, finding some peace while in his garden
An artwork of planning while following the laws of nature and seasons
I'm sure he said a prayer or two as we all do when it comes to surviving in ways we know how
He understood if you take from the earth you must give some back to the earth
For he knew it's a give and take to keep the earth and land for future great harvests
I remind myself of how it is with ethics and higher standards for earth and thee
I wonder how ethics and higher standards have helped me and others in life
As it always can't be your way, maybe it's better with a higher way, like a sustainable way
I wonder and ponder this for me and thee for a greater way.

Rose Lumbaca Crane

Travel on

I can't deny that you don't have to be a gypsy to find your own road -
Your abundance of colour has filled my every desperate window
We've taken our life's journeys in two sets of directions-
those we know, and the one that inevitably follows
Ultimately arriving eternally at a place I will call, for now, our Tomorrow
The crack of sore soles treading on old gravel groves is uneasy, with no compass we've done well my friend,
and we've traveled here both together and alone
Life takes a long time,
whether it felt too fast or achingly goes too slow
in every season and in between every shadow that crawls
I will seek you
Amongst prayers, to the duality of a mystery and fates connection
I will watch entranced for some prediction of my own
I'm needing that version of us, just nearer to each other
So through the expanse of every tangible element and incongruent sense
I will find your amber sun, find our unwritten horizon, and take a chance on the journey
when yours has moved you on to another

Suzanne Siebert

Whitehorse Orchestra strikes up again

"We haven't been
  blown
      scraped
          caressed
             plucked
                struck
                    dampened
For nearly two years."

Excitement hums.

Piccolo furtively pops out of tiny case, sits beside flute sisters,
Ready to add sparkle to those high passages.

Violin cases line walls again,
Their contents tucked under chins, strings tightened and tuned.
Bows move up and down against their cake of rosin,
Releasing sweet pine fragrance.

Violas sneak out of larger cases,
Hoping they won't be butt of yet another viola joke
This morning.

Heavy double basses are laid on their sides,
Covers unzipped,
Then stand tall, naked and proud.

Against the sea of rich timbres

The gold and silver of the brass section shines.
Heraldic horns line up
Beside the bold brash trumpets
While podgy tubas jostle for position
In competition
Against the largest and rowdiest family
The percussion.

Four wide timpani roll out pompously
Are tuned
Ready to lay foundation resonance to the full orchestra.
Snare drum barks out a rhythmic test pattern.
The elegant chimes glide past,
Confident they can add a rich touch to dramatic passages.
Bass Drum nestles in its cradle
Puffing out its chest in anticipation of a booming finale to the piece.
Whip smirks on its stand,
Waiting to leap into action with a crack.

Finally oboe's soulful, long held note – A440!

Let the rehearsal begin.

Roslyn Evans

The silence of water

The English Novelist Virginia Woolf committed suicide in 1941.

The beauty of the world has two edges, one of laughter, one of anguish, cutting the heart asunder.
VW - A Room of One's Own, (1929), Chap 1, p.17

For Moon

Listen
I had finished at last with those words
you will later dissect
I had said enough
lived too often criticised, cosseted, trapped
violated by horrible voices
incessantly consuming my space

to see, know, hear nothing
that was my peace

I left by the back door, dark with rain
made my way quickly
through the years
to the river Ouse
with its promise of silence
I chose the stones carefully
more for their size
than their beauty,
a strange transgression at the end,

and dropped them, one by one
into my pockets for perfect balance,
as you will later know

but what you will not know
was the sound of the sweet bird melody
singing me into my final truth,
and what you cannot know
was the horror of leaving my loved ones,
Leonard, Vanessa, Vita, far behind

and even though you will later
judge me mad
and examine the worlds I created
to find my essence

what you will never know
was even as the water was swallowing my eyes
into peaceful darkness, and bewitching silence
I was thinking of your
misunderstanding

Sandra G Lanteri

Still waters

Still waters erode the copper earth
Twisting and turning beneath the blazing sun
Animals upon the horizon
The mist kisses the sky and floats toward heaven
Clouds form around the mountains
And holds each town dear to their heart
The clarity of cleansing
Liquid full of life
The moon shifts the tides
Breathing new life in to each and every creature
Drop by drop washing away the sins of life

Summertime

Beautiful golden arches cup the horizon line
The warm wind rustles through the kiwi vine
There is such comfort and beauty in being alive
The air fills my lungs and I can finally breathe
All worries and doubts taken by the breeze
First of December the season's begun
Animals and humans all bask in the sun
Crickets chirp and chickens cheep
My eyes flutter closed soon to find sleep

Amanda Divers

The key

She turns her key to a warming home of art where
music plays to every willing ear so many moods and
each plays out its part some tunes stretch far away and
some are near.

And in one room a poet sings her song
to all who choose to enter and be still
for those who play are neither right nor wrong just
there for everyone to take their fill.

She takes her fill and lingers in that place where time
stands still to lift the soaring soul buoyed by the many
facets of time's face; she stays to play her song, at times
to stroll.

This is the way she thinks to live her life — safe yet
exposed, away from petty strife.

Ann Simic

Great Aunt Oriel's ashes

Great Aunt Oriel's ashes resided on a cupboard shelf
Wrapped in a multi coloured beach towel
Under squashed sun hats
And a faded umbrella, I can't lift with age, perished

with age and dust
Waiting twenty years for her event . . .
The day of 'Scattering'.

For this day, a family gathering,
An assortment of relatives
With only vague memories some with none
Of a childless old woman who had all her days,
Lived alone
Behind her dark little second-hand bookshop
At the edge of a little country town.
Great Aunt Oriel! Not true
She was small, her needs were small
That's how she liked things – small.
The box holding her ashes was light.
She was propped under a weeping willow tree
Nearly hidden
So the picnickers were hardly reminded
Of why they had gathered
On that day of the small settling of her soul,
Her glory being the wafting aromas
Of the sausages on the coin-in-the slot barbeque
Sustained by one or two bottles of red
In plastic cups.
The scene became overcast,
Thunder and a flash of lightening

Gusty winds with the threat of rain
That developed into a downpour.
The picnickers cleared up , quickly dispersed,
Driving off one hundred miles to the city
With only hurried goodbyes
While Great Aunt Oriel remained
Reposed, left behind in her box
Under the weeping willow

Months passed before a shabby box arrived
On the doorstep of Oriel's (once removed)
Cousin's eldest nephew.
Great Aunt Oriel was returned
Looking as well as to be expected
Into the unloving arms of family
Traced by a rather smudged name and date
And an undertaker's label.

Judith Dowling

Morning noise, upstairs

The old kettle jingles
are here
are meandering
are contorting their
drooping faces into
groggy smiles.

The elephant thuds upstairs
it speaks in
half-eaten tongues
its laugh is frogspawn
gooey and almost asleep.

Lucy Tomov

Vacant blocks

When I was young I played in vacant blocks
And as I grew up change was everywhere
Stragglers from European battlefields arrived
Italian builders, hot salamis, bricks; sweat dripped through the air.

I'd never heard of garlic until it grabbed hold of me
Couldn't get enough of it sharing lunches in the yard
My parents never cooked with it, like chillies, we had none
Our treat was dipping bread and frying it in lard.

Soon our street was filled with multicultural life
We picked up phrases, styles and fashions
Refugees from Burma taught me how to use my fists
It came in handy playing sport which always was my passion.

I miss the old street more these days thinking back to when
I'd kick a footy down the road and revel in the sun.
I miss the neighbours making chatter, trying to fit in
Back then it seemed uncomplicated. It really felt like fun.

Peter Levy

She is not just . . .

She is not just her long beautiful hair
She is not just her attractive look or her lovely face features

She is not just people's opinions about her
She is not just a stunning sculpture or a breathtaking picture

She is pure glass made out of burning fire
She is a magical angel emanated from massive wreckage

She was an elegant warrior forced to fight in the mire.
she needed unending patience, she needed courage

You don't see the wounds, you don't see the scars
You can just see the glory that shines from her soul

You can see her eager passion to reach the stars
She learnt how to stand up, after each loss, after each fall.

She is simply gorgeous in whole.

Rahaf Al Maalouf

My unkempt hair

My unkempt hair did not bother me when younger
Busy playing outside all day long in the wonder
My hair at times was mistaken for twigs, wheat and wildflowers
For I sometimes played amongst the twigs, wheat and wildflowers
That is how it is meant to be when younger
Even at times when not so much younger
As I was a child of earth, moon and wonder
A child lost at times but found true meaning amongst the twigs, wheat and wildflowers
One day I found a little bird in my hair, I suppose it thought it was a place that looked right
The next thing I knew the little bird would start to talk to me
How could that be? It would tell me many things, many things I needed to hear
To live a life that is true, self-disciplined, rich and daring
If you don't know what's true, seek the truth as that is what you are meant to do
To cherish the earth, sky and others
But I do, I said
How do you do that, said the bird?
I started to wonder and ponder the question the bird asked
Please said the bird don't forget to cherish yourself as there are not many people like you
With hair like twigs, wheat and wildflowers.

Rose Lumbaca Crane

Red brick walls

St Giles' red brick walls
Enclose hundreds of mourners
Listening to Bach's second cello suite.
Notes written with grief
For a young wife and mother
Now throb with grief
For a young husband and father.

How could you chose to leave a world
That aches with such beauty, such music?

A shattered body lies
Beneath his white cassock,
Cross and dove symbol on his chest
Gold sash around his waist.

The celebrant resumes:

"I gazed at the shelves of books
Floor to ceiling in his study.
He tried so hard.
Tried to lift men's spirits,
His own as well."

Young widow hidden in black
Sits alone in front pew,
Too numb to feel,
Too numb to know
How to understand
The Savage God.

Revisited thirty years later,
St Giles' stern brick walls
Are softened with greenery,
Fragrant walkways, overhanging eaves,
Pergola with climbing clematis and hardenbergia.
The February sun, which in 1988 shone so cruelly
Benignly warms community gardens
Sheltered by wall of bright mosaics.
A flock of lorikeets settle noisily in gum tree,
Then wheel and fly off,
A riot of red and green against a blue sky.

Dona Nobis Pacem

Roslyn Evans

On the way to the Tate Modern

This poem first appeared in *Best Australian Poems,*
ed. Les Murray

On the way to the Tate Modern
that damp Sunday morning
with the feeble light piercing the muddy Thames
and the whiffs of stale beer oozing from grimy taverns,
and right near the golden Southwark Cathedral
where the rose tracery of the Great Hall
punctures the ruined air
they followed me,
the lost souls of past eras

quite suddenly
they caught my ignorance unawares
as I walked through the deserted alleyways
and happened upon the Clink Street Prison
the good Bishops of Winchester
had devised, all that long time ago

so easily they had slipped through time
caught in the crevices of greedy injustice,
hanging around plague infested corners
no fiery *Gordon* riots could destroy,
waiting

tapping me on the shoulder
tugging at my heart
creeping into my thoughts
vying for my attention
those Roman thieves

Tudor heretics, and Stuart murderers
those disobedient priests
and noisy drunken actors
together with the *Winchester Geese,*
the wronged, sad, mad whores
freed only for church going

all there that grey Sunday morning
in their iron chains
waiting

and they were my undoing
as I walked the dark lanes alone
followed by a real shadow,
and felt the screams of the damned
the fears of the abused
and the panic of the hopeless,
good, modern Londoners have
long since forgotten

so that the getting there,
the old walk to the new Tate
became more meaningful
more significant
than many of the illusory canvases
pretentious abstractions, and yawning colours
manipulating that gallery's
slick, vacuous space

Sandra G Lanteri

Waters to the sky

As I float upon the opaque illusion of comfort
I am warmed in depth by something as nourishing as it can be ones death
I am held in a midst of below and above, well surrounded by the natural balm
Only from the heavens has this place come to pass
As one drop falls from my eye, one drop falls from the sky
I am weathered and weak yet held by the world of waters deep
Facing all I will never see
As time turns and light fades
I am baptized again by the angels that cry with me
In the pales of their stars making their way across the dark expanse of never knowing
Waters hold me casting my sight towards you
Only because I am floating

Suzanne Siebert

A neighbour's regret

A young woman alone moved into our street
And at least twice a week we would meet
Her nature was pleasing, her face in repose
We chatted of nature and aromas of rose

Over years it was always more of the same
I don't now remember if she mentioned her name
On passing her house I would see her and smile
There was grace in her movements, charm in her style

Her hair turned to snow in the blink of an eye
Mine too, she must have observed passing by

The day of the black car is vivid and clear
Two men wheeled her body, so limp and so dear

Another family moved in but that magic was lost
I'd still stop and chat about value and cost
I was asked "Did you know her? So long in this street."
I said, "Sorry, I didn't," as my heart skipped a beat.

Peter Levy

The Brussels sprout

'I hate Brussels sprouts'
No amount of stabbing with my fork would make it go away,
I was four years old, did as I was told, so there on a chair I had to stay
It looked at me and I looked at it while my father gave one of his talks-
Something about saving babies and eating my sprout
And those poor brown babies in Tanganyika who only ate Wali and Oooganika
Not my mother's Brussels sprouts all sodden and buttered.
I lifted my fork as far as my nose and gave my father my ugliest glare,
My temper rose as I spluttered and muttered--.'It's just not fair'!
I grizzled and groaned till my face was red, then I yelled, 'I wish I was dead'.
So my father threatened to send me to bed.
That made me bolder so over my shoulder, I tossed that Brussels sprout –
Whatever the cost – to the floor, where that terrible sprout looked up at me
And I thought of little brown babies, in Tanganyika ,
Which was way down our street and way around the corner
Passed where the tram line stops where you have to squint to see
If any little Tanganyikan babies are peeping.
I couldn't imagine how I would help them at all
By eating that wretched sprout.

I just knew I could have saved about a hundred or more babies
It was hard to imagine about how it could possibly be
For those little brown babies in Tangyanika
If I'd eaten that Brussels sprout
I wanted for nothing more
Than to catch the tram
Way way down the road to Tanganyika
Where I could eat Wali and Oooganika
And I wouldn't have to eat those sprouts any more.

Judith Dowling

Time on roofs

The roof of my father's garage I would sit and just be
The sun greeting me with its warmth and love
For a time I lived at a place that had a flat roof
On the roof I would go to see the world in a different light
From the view up high I would go to see what else there is for me
Wondering and wishing while on these roofs to see what else there is for me
A place to go and see, what steps to take to lead me to the journey forward
Beyond where I was, what to learn, what to experience
I would dance and dine on roofs where the light and food was fine
I would see people bath on roofs, some would contemplate their lives on roofs,
I would exercise on roofs,
I like having breakfasts on roofs to start the day
I found myself on the highest roof of the world one day, the Himalayas
Such wonder and awe of being there on the highest roof of this world
I like being on roofs as by night I was a bit closer to the stars
Oh how I wanted to be a star, a star of stage and screen for just a while
And of course I would wish upon a star while being on the roofs.

Rose Lumbaca Crane

Rhapsody on old lovers

How many songs and poems
From when time began
Try to capture the mystery
Of lovers' meeting?
But no words can tell
The passion that flares,
Burns and burns more brightly
With each passing year.
The bodies' shapes change.
What used to be possible
Is replaced with new ways
Of being close,
Delighting in each others' existence,
Scaling new heights of intensity,
And new depths of peace
In each others' arms.

Roslyn Evans

Trampoline

Our multi-faceted world is changing shape again
Sharp angles are replacing once rounded certainties
and there is a closing in
with the expanding space of loss

After a rushed birthday meal for a six-year-old,
fish and chips and ice-cream cake
for, who has time to cook

come the solemn words
floating over the discarded balloons
paper hats, fairy bread, spent candles

come the sobering thoughts
that allow no room for misinterpretation

terminal, accident, cancer, stroke, heart
school mates, work colleagues,
gym buddies, bloke next door

A whirlpool of memories rising then
of remember when, what might have been, if only
who is left?   who is next?

while outside
joyful children jump higher and higher
on the birthday trampoline,
screaming the vitality of new life

Sandra G Lanteri

Magpie friend

The world had transformed
Shrunk to the perimeter of the house

How to live without my friends?
Without the casual hi, the comforting hug, the coffee chat

And then, like a mysterious gift,
A new friend came to the back door
In a flurry of black and white
Wings beating, eyes glinting
Head cocked curiously
As if to say, I'll be your friend in your isolation

This curious magpie, with the one eye
Seemed as lonely as I felt
We sat in comfortable silence,
Me with my book, my feathered friend primping, singing, observing

And now the world comes again to life
My friends and I meet up once more
But somehow my winged companion has vanished,
Where to I'll never know
I miss her more than I would have thought.

Sharon Hurst

The ever monster

I look back and love that little girl
Who took the hand of a monster.
Into the back of a derelict shed
To save a kitten . . .
A kitten that wasn't there. . .
Nor indeed was that lovely Madonna
Enshrined amidst a garden of lilies
In the golden frame that hung on her bedroom wall.
Protecting her, they said.
Instead . . .
coarse hairy arms
Hands with stumpy fingers engrained with dirt.
Guttural breathing, catarrhal spitting.
The obscene belly,
The colour, the shape, the smell
Of a bag of stinking potatoes.
Marauding over her body
Shaking the balance of her mind.
I look back and love that little girl
My self – with flying plaits, rosy cheeks,
And a home at the top of the hill.
The little girl who escaped a monster
Only to forever wear bruises.
She had bitten that monster face with all her might
Shuddering with the force.
She had pushed her knuckles
Into its rheumy-eye sockets
And kicked its buckled legs
As she dragged at its hair
Stagnant with grease.
That monster- a lumbering fool,

The child – my self, small, quick, clever
Broke through a battered door
Into the light of day.
There were no screams
No gentle Madonna's arms,
Instead only rasping sounds from her throat.
As she fled.
I look back and love that little girl
Stumbling, tripping, stumbling again
Feet tangling
In the rags of the tartan skirt
The monster had ripped from its bodice.
She heard a cacophony of madness,
Springtime magpies at her head.
Scratching, squabbling,
Swooping down from the fine
Branches of a river gum
Pecking at her head.
Blood smeared her face,
Mixed with dried monster blood
Down her cheek, seeping into her mouth . . .
Forever the sickening taste of fear
Forever the colour of shame.
I look back and love that little girl.

Judith Dowling

Custodians

I swagger through the parkland
I know I'm not alone
a constant hand is on my shoulder
my guide from where, unknown.

The peace of ancient wisdom
lingers thick within the air
eyes of custodians, warriors
in still unbroken stare.

How could I possibly understand
the trust they put in me
to keep land the way it was
always meant to be

A council from beyond
each in perfect harmony
careful steps that harm no life
that echo tree to tree.

Another shiver slowly passing
though not one ounce of fear
I am but a stranger
more a bumbler, here.

If trees could talk, if rocks could write
give lessons for this lonely night
I'd fix the wrongs and understanding
I'd make all things here right.

But I have none of all that stuff
I stumble, shaken with the cold
I fail to see what lies in my path
or hear when truths are told.

Peter Levy

Want

I want to criss-cross centuries
to contemplate the complexities
passion, torment, beauty
and mystery of the creative spirit

I want to be Vermeer's pearl earring
Wagner's Flying Dutchman
Hepworth's chisel
and Vasari's Arezzo pen

I want to escape The Leads with Casanova
ride into battle with Joan
carry Mona Lisa to Amboise
and dine at Stein's Parisian table

I want to walk Florence with the Brownings
play the sax with Coltrane
be Matisse's scissors, and
read Eliot as Smart paints Labyrinth

I want to stroll the Shoalhaven with Boyd
sit with Traill at the bridge
roam Baynton's bushland
gather the discarded with Gascoigne
and live on Winton's Cloudstreet

then with Austen's pride, and no prejudice at all
I want to ride freely with Mr. Darcy,
which just might help me understand
the creative process best of all

Sandra G Lanteri

Senses

I sense you taking off, beside me
Lying in the darkness- waiting for eternity to take you
Hand holding hand, until the end, just as I said I would
Breathing in a last deep breath, and letting it fall
If everything else was amiss, and all I could do for you was one thing
It would be giving all the love in our lifetimes, on your forehead my last kiss.
I see nothing and hear less, my memory is my substance,
All that is external is not held tightly because angels fly
The five senses limit me
So I send them goodbye letters, thanking them for their time,
Knowing that even though you are leaving for somewhere better
I am here to sense you taking off, beside me

Suzanne Siebert

The lament of loss

Loss is a tiny four-letter word
Yet it carries the weight of our own sadness
The world's sadness

Once I had loving parents
Their encircling arms and soft words
The boundary of my small child's world.
They are lost . . . forever

Once I had a small, half-blind magpie friend
At the door she'd sing and eat from my hand
She has gone now . . . lost to me.

For seven years my beloved neighbors
Brought joy and comfort to my life
Time's up . . . they have moved on
The fence between our houses is greyer and droops

Once we had boundless freedom
An unwelcome sickness stole that away
And, as if one cataclysm gave permission for more,
I heard the distant rumble of global disaster

Once the world felt safe . . . predictable, and known
Now I know nothing - certainty is lost
Maybe never even there
It would be better to lose all delusion, and just face it:
We win by being born into this world
But ultimately all ends in loss.

Sharon Hurst

www.ingramcontent.com/pod-product-compliance
Lightning Source LLC
Chambersburg PA
CBHW030303010526
44107CB00053B/1803